Additional Praise:

"Thompson's book is, despite what many would have us believe, an American story. It is about the power to make oneself over, to build on the rubble of the past something new, better, more. Throughout this achingly beautiful collection, Thompson falls apart and comes back together again, over and over and over in a brutal reshaping, diving into tsunami waves to come out the other side, themselves. An essential read."

– Eirinie Carson, author of *The Dead Are Gods*

"This life / my life / that chose me / gave me a blessing in swallowing me whole," Thompson writes in *A Congregation of Alligators*, a poetry collection that meditates inside the wreckage and wonder of becoming. Thompson's poems are generous—an offering of forgiveness with teeth—extending tenderness to all those, including the self, in the aftermath.

– Hieu Minh Nguyen, author of *This Way to the Sugar*

"A writer's responsibility is to create a world so undeniable that the reader has no option but to see themselves within it. In *A Congregation of Alligators,* Thompson accomplishes just that. Each poem is both question and answer to queer resilience, joy and determination. A reminder to look at the miles of grief without blinking, leaving mistakes in a big font for those seeking to find themselves in poetry."

– Yesika Salgado, author of *Corazón*

A CONGREGATION OF ALLIGATORS

Grayson Thompson

Copyright © WRITE BLOODY

All rights reserved. No part of this book may be used, performed, or reproduced in any manner whatsoever without written permission from the publisher except in the case of brief quotations embodied in critical articles or reviews.

First edition. 2025
A Congregation of Alligators
Grayson Thompson, 2025
ISBN: 978-1-949342-79-6
Publisher: Write Bloody Publishing
Edited By: Haley Hutchinson
Proofread by: Sam Rose Preminger
Cover Designed by: Derrick Brown
Interior Layout by: Derrick Brown
Type set in EB Garamond

*"...I think you mean what you say
when you say you want to stay alive..."*

-Lucy Dacus

PART I: THE PRE-REQUISITE COURSES

ALIVE WITH NO ASTERISK..7
IN THE MORNING AND AMAZING...9
LETTER OF RECOMMENDATION..11
SECONDHAND EMBARRASSMENT...14
THE 7-ELEVEN AFTER 9/11
AND EVERY WAR AFTER CHILDHOOD..16
IN YOUR 20S, NO KID GLOVES ON..20
I DIDN'T KNOW LOVE UNTIL I KNEW NICKELBACK..................21
FROM THE VIEW OF THIS FIGHT,
I SEE SIERRA NEVADA FOOTHILLS..22
OUR TOOTHBRUSHES AND OTHER GERMS.................................23
SOCIAL MEDIA IS A HYMNAL OF GOSPEL HOOKS....................25
WITH THE WEIGHT OF SINKING SHIPS..26
MA, TELL YOUR FRIENDS...28
A GIRL CRIED IN PATWA SO A BOY CAN LIVE 30
WHERE DID YOU GO IN ALL THE CONFUSION?.........................34
I LOVE YOU (THE WAYS WE RESTRICT
AND THE WAYS WE STARVE)..37
GOD IS A TRANSWOMAN...41

PART II: NATIVE TONGUE IS MADNESS

PHONE TAG WITH THE ANXIETY SPIRAL......................................45
DUFFEL BAG..46
CANVAS CANOPY STAR SHELTERING THE BEGINNING.........48
THE COMET...50
IN A MAN-MADE LAKE IN AN OFFICE PLAZA.............................52
ORANGE, PREVIOUSLY CALLED "YELLOW-RED",
AND ALL WORDS AFTER WARNING...55
PANTOUM UNDER THE ROBIN WILLIAMS TUNNEL.................56
OFFERING FROM THE ALIEN..57

PART III: A LONG WAY FROM FLORIDA

CUVIER'S BEAKED WHALES HOLD THE RECORD
FOR LONGEST BREATH HELD..61
THIS IS A POEM FOR PEOPLE WHOSE MOTHERS
FORGET THEIR BIRTHDAYS...63
INTERSTELLAR 67
SISTERS...69
ME: A COUNTRY..72
(ZOMBIE POEM) ALL THESE LINES WERE KILLED
TO MAKE SOMETHING YOU'D LIKE 74
CONVERSATION WITH MY ESTRANGED BROTHER
BEFORE HURRICANE MILTON..76
WHAT IT'S LIKE TO BE A STEALTHY FAG..77
ODE TO BLACK BOYS, PREVIOUSLY BLACK GIRLS, CALLED OREOS...........78
QUEER, AS IN, MY BACKBONE IS...80

PART IV: MY BODY & OTHER STORIES PUT TO REST

BANNERLINE RINGLEADER...84
GRAYSON..85
MY 9YR OLD NIECE TOLD ME SHE KNOWS WHAT A HAIKU IS..................88
THE BOY WHO DJS THE RIVER..90
PORTRAIT OF DATING MEN..92
FROM THE THERAPY ROOM...93
UPON LEARNING MY FAVORITE PLANET IS THE ONLY ONE WITH A HEART
(TOMBAUGH REGIO)...94
MY LAST GRANDFATHER HAS DIED...96
ELECTION (S)KIN..98
THE BLOWER'S CHILD...99
NOAH AND KATELYN'S LATE WEDDING POEM..................................101
JOY CAME AFTER THE PRE-REQUISITE COURSES................................103
CUÍDASE, MAS O MENOS..106
MY MOM MAY READ MY POEMS
AND NOT KNOW HOW TO BE PROUD OF ME.....................................108

PART I: THE PRE-REQUISITE COURSES

ALIVE WITH NO ASTERISK

Sometimes the body needs
to be altered
and it does not
have to mean
anything

about us,
about panic
or about pain.

Sometimes our bodies
are just vessels
we want to feel in.

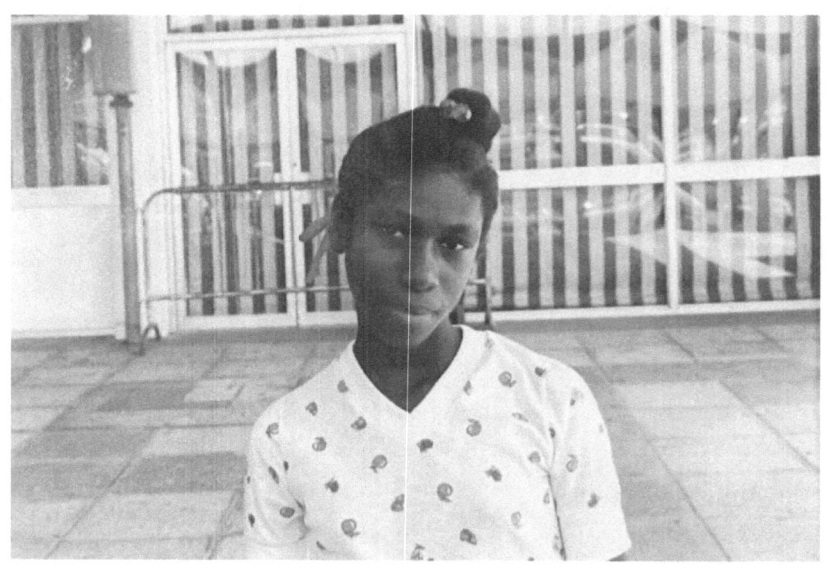

(My mother, as a little girl in Jamaica)

My mother lived through one of the bloodiest political elections in the country's modern history only to hold my hand, around the same age as she had been, as we escaped from NYC on the day the Twin Towers fell. My mother was separated from her mother as a teenager, a country between them, and wouldn't be reunited for almost 10 years. My mother—misunderstood by her whole family, told in so many ways she didn't fit—survived and said "enough" to every awful man. A single mother, she raised four children.

My mother and I grew up together.
Her life could never have prepared either of us
for the congregation of alligators
I would have to put to rest.

Remember this little girl,
hold her and everything she had to carry.

IN THE MORNING AND AMAZING

I don't know how ▮▮▮▮ I have met myself
a song long, ▮▮▮▮ ghost pencil ▮▮▮▮ portrait ▮▮
▮▮▮▮▮▮ my lives burned through camera reels
all of them filled with white ▮▮▮ white ▮▮▮▮ white ▮▮
▮▮▮▮ the inside of an anthill,
an army of people teeth out ready to undo me.

This ride
took me here,
looking at you,

leaving the length of my ▮▮▮▮
to drown on the lawn
for all of us—
everyone that knew loving me
was never meant to break ▮▮▮▮

It wasn't easy.
It wasn't clean.
It took a lot
of starting over.
                        Yes, I know
                                      there will be
                                      more times I will have
                                      to start over

The moment ▮▮▮▮ fell,
▮▮▮▮ wild and breaking,
god honest, should have been
where I stopped

pulling punches on my true stories
for fear ▮▮▮▮▮▮▮
where my "I love you's"
weren't weaponized with running away.

LETTER OF RECOMMENDATION

To Whom It May Concern:

The person you are about to meet escaped
thinking himself into a coffin,
ate playing small
for breakfast,
took his character out
for lunch;
a graffiti of slack-jawed, grass-grasping
grief.

He held everything dear
in a trash bag,
graduated
to a blue suitcase
running for the outline of home.
Took years to know it
was the shape of his body.

This is a safety assessment
of where he's been.
He didn't want a hug, but
wanted to be crushed.

He tells people he misses them,
that he loves them,
with no expectation of return.

To love him
means to understand
that it hurt to get here,

that it broke him
like a re-interpretation
of a book you thought was truth.

When I think of my childhood, I imagine it like this scene. My soccer team award ceremony, winning two awards, a stone-faced hilarity wearing a hot pink 101 Dalmatians shirt paired with baby blue and white pants. Trying to fit "boy" into "girl," trying to fit a family's pride into two statues and a straight face.

SECONDHAND EMBARRASSMENT

There was a crowd
crying mercy for riverbed bones and
you wore earplugs
the size of resentment.

I spent my weight in pens drawing
strength from the back
of my knees,
back of my throat,
the murmur of the train past Bunker Hill

is that what life made your body? A bunker?
is that the sound it gave my heart?

born pending, the forgiveness

is the only casualty
I'm bringing home to rest.
Risked it on terror,
the pain I ate
with my eyes.

Painted
a black and white dust-
bowl, dodged the montage of anvils
impaling me from the sky,
replayed the grooves of my brain
filled with lynched letters
vinyl-skipping like broken water when they strung up

your name.

There is a world that burns
like embarrassing memories
in the way we used to live.

The war should have ended
the first time someone looked at me
like a slow-motion daydream.

It should have been called off before I ran
until there was no more me to run out of.

Now I know what it feels like to be
someone's exhale, what they rummage for
in the dark
for rescue.

THE 7-ELEVEN AFTER 9/11 AND EVERY WAR AFTER CHILDHOOD

where I had my first Slim Jim

after the FAA forced all planes to ground
My family
every prayer
in smoke plume
suicide

my grandfather
waiting to be buried
in Florida, waiting
for me

every quiet whisper on alert
I looked for god in the clouds
Ma promised he was there
said to say my bedtime prayer

If I should die
before I awake
I pray the Lord
my soul to take

twenty-three years later
wandering in a hellscape
where my friends live
in a protest.

in protest
is where you'll find

the most people per square mile
committed to being right

a teenager asked me
Were you alive on 9/11?
What was it like?

It was confirmation
of what it feels like
to live in a world

where children cannot trust
adults to keep them safe

No more mangos
with my grandfather

who never told me to dress
like a girl

There is a child
crying everywhere
in every edge of the sky
in a school
a war
the mirror
between gang graffiti
the dance team with skintight leotards
and the boys under the skirt
the doctor's office
Jack and Coke
overdose
bathroom toilet

text left on read
dad's dead
mom's dead
scarred
starved
controlled
this body
food pantry
needles and escape
highway exit
hit and run
car gasket
OG Kush
homeless encampment
home
hormone
inside ourselves

There is a child crying.
There is a child crying.
There is a child.
There is,

and we will always
make it about something else.

Chris (left) was my oldest cousin. When this photo was taken, he was in the Navy and docked for a moment in Massachusetts and our family was able to see him. This photo was taken during the time of 9/11. My family and I boarded a plane on 9/11, leaving New York to fly to my grandfather's funeral. Panicked people, news on the little plane TVs, I asked my mom in a too-loud kid voice about the pilot killing us. My mom told me I was safe, told me to pray. My mom, like she was behind this photo, can convince the air to stand still in the cold.

IN YOUR 20S, NO KID GLOVES ON

I was not born a punishment.
Being understood made me angry,
██████ I was in love with being a mystery to myself.

██ There isn't an after.
████ Everything that's better is right here.
Look at me
robbing the sky ████
turning it silver,
laughing in fluent magic.

██████ All these colors lost
in the back of someone's warning sign,
████████████████████

their hips, their mouths,
the way they looked ████ in the night
of their rooms.

If we'd met 10 years ago
████████████
I ██████ a snake charmer
and afraid of the dark,
you ██████ in love
with all the me's I would never become,
you'd miss that I was ██████
a ██████ blackout
screaming ████
when no one
was around.

I DIDN'T KNOW LOVE UNTIL I KNEW NICKELBACK

Not until I heard them in the trailer
off a goat farm in Maine

peddling the summer
through haunted bike parks,

running my boyness to the gas station,
learning to drive a car
into the brush.

You don't know
the meaning of a photograph
until you don't remember the person in it—
their silhouette, a bear den
dragging every dead thing in.

The back of your hair
has bobbed through
every crowd in my mind,
holding candles to lip balm,
burning kisses into skin,

singing in karaoke boxes,
romanced in a condensation coated window,
tongue pulsing the mic,
holding space for a fringed-jean music video

believe me, I didn't know myself.
Never used to being wanted.
Never knew how it would taste.

FROM THE VIEW OF THIS FIGHT, I SEE SIERRA NEVADA FOOTHILLS

What's all that blue shit up there?
You said,
Baby, that's the sky.

A laugh as big as my loneliness.
A covering I can't shake.
Thank you for telling me
you're not happy.

My heart, a broken trail,
boot prints and baby feet—
remember how those folks
asked us for directions
to the falls?
Green and cold
like my cave learning
the echo your name made
for the first time.

All our answers laced
with half expectations. Who
would trust us?

A portrait of gold fading.
A canary call of a time
when every left turn took us home.

OUR TOOTHBRUSHES AND OTHER GERMS

Don't tell me
you ran out of words
for autumn.

Tell me there are spiders
in my death-cab
of a Ford Fiesta.

Tell me
the throat irritation
is from the bedroom fan

that's been collecting memories
since the day we escaped
from the apartment with mold for walls

and not an anaphylactic episode caused by the Trader Joe's ice
cream cones I eat
(literally every night).

Tell me mashed potatoes
are used as the base for many desserts
and you want to exclusively date
at classic American chain restaurants like Applebee's or Legal
Seafood.

Tell me
you've been eating chips in bed.
You hit the garage frame
with your car
again.

Tell me that
there's nothing wrong with me,

that I'm not a coastline
colliding your life with my fog.

I'll stop apologizing
for being here.
I'll tell every wounded thing I'm sorry.

I'm sorry.

I'll start collecting all the floss
I leave as reminders
that I was here,

won't complain
about the crumbs,
the elephant mug
holding our toothbrushes and other germs
that don't bother you,

how you leave every room with the lights on.

Tell me anything
before you say
you ran out of words for falling

in love with me.

SOCIAL MEDIA IS A HYMNAL OF GOSPEL HOOKS
*(in response to hearing another beautiful word from
Alok Vaid-Menon)*

Love is a conviction
that looks back at us
from between the shapes
our eyes make in the dark.

Some of us make sense of it with apologies.
Others, shame
beamed here from the crack of stars
so messy
mothers had to learn to bend.

Children teach their parents
lessons they didn't know they needed to learn.

I materialized so full
that my mother couldn't catch the lessons
god left.

I heard this week
that *love lacerates*
and it's worth it.

There's no purpose in holding together
something meant to burst and leak
all over anything that was supposed to
make sense,

like forever.

WITH THE WEIGHT OF SINKING SHIPS

When I present myself at your feet
know that I mean it with every barefoot step.

Jesus in the ballpark
holds me at the belly,
soft spots pierced with stone.

A pool with a broken waterfall
more grill than grass
catching bass on the bank,
hunting in the night,
wrapping ourselves in blankets
around glass tables.

I'm with the boys and
we're growing into our chests.
Mine was a million-dollar shotgun barrel
loaded with longing

unloading blanks into air like
a calling, each breath a burnt shell,
each yell a whistle for the moon.

When I smile the sun to sleep,
believe me I didn't mean to run away,

didn't mean to go missing.
It had everything to do with
taking myself out of the character of perfection.

I was lying

when I said I didn't mean to wring your neck.
I should've said

you were the last story
of worthlessness
I was in love with telling
myself,

playing small,
cellophaning through so many mouths,
snuffing out the oxygen in every one of their syllables
for mercy.

Back then, if I met myself in a dark alley
it would have been the West Side Story,
knifing everything I couldn't let go of
pound for pound,
on display for tickets
at the butcher's shelf.

When you collect me
for your number,
remember a nightlight.

Don't look at me with wet eyes.
Tell me how easy it was
to find me.

Tell me looking at me
felt like a heavyset dream,
a wall of books
you bought just to look at
—something pretty.

MA, TELL YOUR FRIENDS

your granddaughter
once described my job
as helping people cry.

And you're right,
I will often choose the harder way,

but someone real smart
told me the other day

that I move with integrity.
Such choices don't come easy.

Tell them my value
has walked me farther
than any straight-to-voicemail.

I've been beyond hell.
It's not a place.

It's hating yourself.

I didn't know that—
fair warning,
I don't know everything.

Tell them I took in anything anyone would give,
took a microscope to my insides,
wondered if there was anything left.

Extra-life quarter

at the bottom of my left lung,
I had to climb down my throat,
scrape every sad sentence out
and wear myself from the inside for a while.

I wore my best shoes
to life
with every job description written
across my body.

What a beautiful thing I made.
My body
and other vacancies
I left on the floor.

A GIRL CRIED IN PATWA SO A BOY CAN LIVE

On this futon,
I'm a dead star.

My first body
was the bottom of the food chain,
learned from predators

who mashed mounds
that grew women out of scraped knees.

They grinded my girlhood to rubble
with a smile so sharp buildings bled.

Taught me the amount of people my mind can become
is a drinking game for every ignored *no*.

I was all boys hidden in peaches,
an ocean of drowning baboons.
A monster's putting makeup on in the bathroom.

We're all afraid of something.

I've leveled my chest with a thundering of knives;
my woman is six pounds removed.

Been studied from a well of wet eyes
deep-throated buckets of irises.
Made myself a light switch
in the tunnel.

When I am lost
in the emptiness of morning streetlights,
I open my mouth and
every breath
a sun whistle;
every cry,
the answer to relief.

If I can be two places at once
for a song as long as the saddest sentence,
I'd stand between the border of who I was and who I am
singing
echoing melodies
on and off like direction indicators
for the rest of my life.

A name is only our parents' feelings.
It was never a beginning.
It is not the answer to birth,
take it or leave it behind.

I created myself in a chatbox,
wanted Amazing Grace to be my parents,
a landscape of synesthesia,
a choir song ripped from the gutter.

I am a dawn of morning glories
fallen when there's no one around.
Every trip, a reminder of how badly the Earth needs me.

Love
is knowing
that our biggest feelings come
from the sound a door makes when it closes—

my closet,
my bedroom,

my mom's house.

When you come to the door,
knock on me
real hard.

Listen.

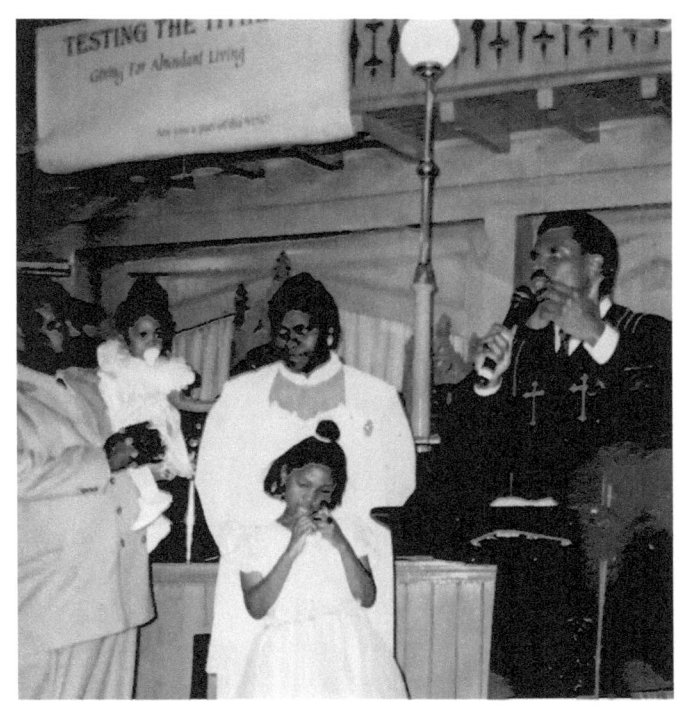

WHERE DID YOU GO IN ALL THE CONFUSION?
(After Johan Harstad)

When I last saw you
we walked a three-mile perimeter in San Francisco.
You had twenty pounds of weight on your back,
winced with each exhale,
breaking for Mexico.

A couple weeks before,

your brother jumped out of a building.

I miss the way you talk.
I felt the home of my name in your voice.

You've been gone over four years now.
You vanished to the desert until you lost yourself
in the snow,
where the beginning and end lives.

I woke up this morning to a haunting—
you skinny-faced, drawn mouth open,
looking like hell and holy water in a mosquito net
somewhere in the woods around Bend.

Your shoes are four sizes bigger.
It's twenty miles to the nearest water.
If you walk yourself out of your skin,

take me with you.

When you asked me what it was like living after a suicide,

I told you I still return to them,
faces to scale on the backdrop of my eyes,
AM radio set to golden hour.

I miss the tiniest things from all the ways I've been left behind—
      room temperature sausage mixed with hot oatmeal,
      flipping miniature skateboards with fingers,
      laughing on repeat in D.C.—

losing someone
lives in our feet.
That's why they call it a pilgrimage.
The sadness flips your mouth into misunderstandings.

I can't promise this life pardons.
I've also fauceted tears from my face in the shape of ampersands
while reading the back of the cereal box,
distracting myself from the sound of the spoon missing the
bowl.

In therapy school
there isn't a class
on what to do when someone we love kills themself
or drinks until the lights black out of their eyes
or when the love of your life leaves you

or

We try remembering somewhere to help compass,
find land
on a planet
moving faster than an inhale
when life has made contusions out of its point.

If you come back home
maybe the first thing that jumps out
will be your brother's name,
maybe it'll be
I'm sorry.

Whatever comes,
I hope it knows there's no way to make sense
of the worst delivered to us.
You don't need anyone's permission
to stay gone.

The leaving
just happens,
especially to the best of us.

If I ever come back
I hope whatever comes out can see
I made it a long way from Florida.

That I am a lesson
transmitted by some long-lost satellite
on a trajectory for the answer
someone forgot they were looking for,

and when it comes
I hope it leaves the rage.

I LOVE YOU (THE WAYS WE RESTRICT AND THE WAYS WE STARVE)

Each one comes with two tortillas
folding my depression
under the raw weight
of onions and cilantro,

witnessing me in neon,
bathed in holy LED on the projection of a parking lot
where I cried alone in the car.

I've always been scared of food poems.
They're always romances—
saliva and glee,
brow sweat and hunched
over benches,
rolled up sleeves.

This poem is portion control and
I can't let the weight I carried here get the best of me.
The center of the sucker
without chewing,
keeping patience,
keeping this smallest part of life
together.

After my stepfather went to sleep
I hid food in the trash can
wrapped in paper towels,
tucked in paper cups flipped upside down.

He wouldn't let us leave the table

until there was a wasteland of crumbs,
a dining table lit up by the stove light
coloring me in a static Dijon.

My mother worked the late shift,
brother in our room laughing at cartoons.
He was big enough to eat two of us,
but my plates were always full.
My dishes collected tears—
bully beef and onions
on repeat,

expected it like Sunday church
like our Massachusetts winters
like his fists.

Some people think we repeat things
because we love them,
but we do it because it feels good
to know what's coming next.

When a person loses all of their energy
the sensitivity of their taste buds increases.
I learned
that our food is more likely to taste better
when we eat in front of mirrors.

It took years to let my reflection keep me company,

to stop ducking him in hallways,
boxing myself into submission,

terrified to bear witness to how much I've grown
to scale.

Memories and mumble brook tears
aged into my face like glass chips.

One of the holiest things a human can feel is hunger,
formed in our first kick,
first holler out the womb.

I thought I started and ended the same:
a song welcoming a child.
Me, the child thought to have never come out right.

Mom,
I was born to bite off more life than I can chew.
I didn't plan on being naked,
dish empty
without the muscles to consume our family.

When the people who raise you can't love you,
you become a walking famine,
spending lifetimes with apologies
moving through you
like whispers,

trying to get filled in any way
you can take it.

I raised a garden above everything that runs on hopelessness.
I know what it feels like to grow out of a reaping.
I know there are more delicious things than hating this life.

A child and a chicken nugget,
eyes wide like the beginning,
showing us all how good it feels to eat.

I am a sand-bodied Florida boy
who learned mercy isn't only found in stillness.
Some alligators can starve themselves for up to three years—
I was born to be here.

A group of them, called a congregation,
taught me hallelujahs are prehistoric.
Been here longer than I've known.

A dawn of morning glories painted across my chest,
love and death in a single day,
lilies across my heart,
a dare to love me
with so much flavor
so when you look at me, you have cravings.

We can wipe the slate clean at 11:59.
One minute short of me knowing what's coming next.

GOD IS A TRANSWOMAN
("This is an apology letter to the both of us / for how long it took me to let things go" —Buddy Wakefield)

In a past life,
I made love to monsters
and melted into skeletons,

imprinted flowers on myself
because one time I went to a scent-sensitive party
where no one wore adornments
and these bodies smelled
like fear.

In this life,
I don't hide anymore,
even when they tried
to kill me.

I am who hackers had in mind
when they decided on anarchy—

the creature of light and dark,
the bitch with stilettos for eyes.

Don't forget me

and the way I took all hope
with me when I walked.

There is a house in my dreams
with two kids and a man who welcomes me
with homemade sweet tea.

He rescues kids from conversion therapy
and black and brown babies
from microwave-ready pain.
He drives a school bus with a plow at the front
and Christmas lights constellating the inside;

his neighbors provide the fuel.

When he saved the last kid
from the last moment
of stripping kids of their magic,
he parked the bus in his driveway,
kept all the lights on.

Now, we choose to leave
our umbrellas at home.
We say the thing.
And I will keep the lights on,
ready at ignition
to show up here with room
on my plate for you.

In the meantime,
have some tea.
I'll tell you about the apology letter to the both of us,
being a writer, and moonlighting
as a becoming.

I'll tell you how to make love stay.

PART II: NATIVE TONGUE IS MADNESS

PHONE TAG WITH THE ANXIETY SPIRAL

I'm sorry // I miss you // I'm anxious // been bingeing a docuseries / about people who escape // taking notes // been trying to call you // to check if you're alive // happy belated birthday by the way / call you back / I was sleeping // starting new meds // so tired // my psychologist didn't call back // we missed each other // I tried to kill myself // took us a while to get through that // been meaning to bring it up // I had shitty friends / wonder if they'd believe me // I don't hold it against them // good to hear you / you okay // can you talk // I'm scared / seeing a new psychiatrist // stressed about not making / my favorite band's listeners this year // last year I was in the top 0.1% and // the year's almost over // and I haven't been listening to much music lately // and everything sounds the same //

Is that a side effect?

DUFFEL BAG

When I was in grad school ▮▮▮
killed himself over the summer.

We shared a bathroom
and he would wrap his towel around his chest,
a shelter. Hair wet, body lean.
Taught me that not all men
wrap secrets around their waists.

My transness, normal.

He was from Texas,
mixed his breakfast sausage in with his oatmeal.

My room sat across from his,
so when our doors opened
we'd catch glimpses into each other's hinging lives.

Mine—strung together with stars.
His—near empty,
a desert standoff.
He only brought a duffel bag.

The Texan obituary painted depression
like something that snatched him like
adding more water to humid air,
like it came without warning.
Parents said it "prohibited" his future.

I would've sat with him
getting picked apart by mosquitoes.
I would've said,

I know what it feels to be swallowing planets,
trying to fill a hollow
that sleeps with you every night.
It can feel like staring Pluto in the face,
holding a galaxy of lonely
in the spaces behind your lungs,
trying with all your atoms to save yourself
from the exhale.

CANVAS CANOPY STAR SHELTERING THE BEGINNING
(In response to "Fat Girl Wants Love" by Yesika Salgado)

I am
- Black
- Queer
- Transgender
- Loved

None of these combinations
will save me from death
or reduce the risk of danger.

I am Black and queer,
a teenager.
The supervisor at my summer job
volunteers to do my hair,
make me feminine.

Their offer reflects my queerness,
a negative correlation of role model.

Don't confuse the children.

I am transgender and queer and Black.
A trans woman in my community dies
my first year of college—
the grief is confusing.
It spirals me in shame.

I am queer and I am Black,
a middle schooler
undone in weekly meetings

with Jehovah Witnesses.

I am queer and I am transgender
and I am in love.
Been told I am the best of both worlds.
Been hidden in catacombs of humiliation.
Been made a cancellation of community
for not being more of this
when there was no more of me
to give.

I am loved
while Black
and queer
and trans.

My niece
asked if hormones can heal.

My best friend flew from Seattle
to spend a week in suburbia
because there's no such thing
as too much sad.

A lover puts a hand on my chest
as I read poems by LED lamp.

I am a holy ghost beacon
in the dark

for every lost deer
gunning for home.

THE COMET

I wonder if the years you tried splitting yourself
from any lingering pieces of me

created your daughter,
who wishes me a Happy Father's day,

asks if you're a father,
asks if I'm a good person,
after you turn her into a teardrop.

It is true:
When softness is identified

there will be a man to take aim,

not expecting the debris of possibility
to coat him in everything he can't be.

To be in proximity of my love
and not deserve it

is a severance paid in rage.

I understand the weight
of grieving me.

You weren't meant to come out alive

from all the ways I am bigger than this body,

outgrowing the hateyourself forced into my childhood.

For the people whose families can't hold them,
we were born to swim

like a congregation of alligators,
each dinosaur breath so holy
the stars opened the sky.

IN A MAN-MADE LAKE IN AN OFFICE PLAZA
(after reading the article: *Alien Remains Found in Mexico*)

Homeless people bathe as I watch
from the window
while playing board games
with children that still believe in magic
for right now's living.

For right now's living,
I hear about what the worst of us can do
to children and shrink
the Peter Pan who shadows them,
fill the tunnels of my ears.

Propelled with blood, the smaller me bare-
knuckles my notes to the dissociation pile
in my mind.

To forget what hurts
about what I do for a living,
I brand my eardrums
with every question about the difference between
"just talking" and "go together."
The "you might not know this show" (it's literally *Naruto*)
and "oh, you listen to Biggie?"

The light of halos
that whistle every dark word,
the boy who cried for one hour
telling me that *He's a private person*—

I bury the trauma of being a therapist

with conspiracy conversations about alien remains with my friends,
laugh with my bestie Kari through shuffled, cackling words.

These aliens were
Latino,
outsiders,
brown-skinned—
unsurprising.

Of course, found by Latinos.
More a reason for the worst of us
to say,

You don't belong here.
You are alien.
Here is proof
from your own mouth.

I bury to the base of my bagpipe;
I was told once that's where tears live.
I haven't thought about my forgotten inner child,
haven't thought about her in years.

The girl who hooked people's leftovers,
waiting to be rescued from the balcony
filled with hoarded things.

I was a pretty woman and
this is filthy work:

unhinging my jaw the length of the alphabet
to plant tombstones for their monsters in my gums,

every *I'm here*
nutrients for the Earth.

I was made to reconcile the secrets of cemeteries
and today,
this pain was not worth it,
the children were not worth it—

To wake up, again,
3:41 AM,
curl into a suicide
when the worst of us
starts burning the wildflowers
from my brain.

My most used word
the year I shed my shame and ran
was "serendipitous."

There is no hopelessness in tomorrow,
there is only The Peg House
in Leggett, California
off Highway 101
where somebody loves me,
where the motto is "Never Don't Stop."

ORANGE, PREVIOUSLY CALLED "YELLOW-RED", AND ALL WORDS AFTER WARNING

There are better things to bruise here
than our feelings,

there are lines that need bleeding,
a dead antler of a summer.

Your mama will remember
every picture of you I sent her,

but she doesn't need to know
what you say to yourself
when the surface of the water licks back
all that's left.

You and I,
a church rainbow of books
trying to make a marriage out of the shelves.

There are words as round as orange
filling every sound in cry,
moving through us so fast
they erase our fingertips.

Surrender.
Mercy.
Family.

Come home.

PANTOUM UNDER THE ROBIN WILLIAMS TUNNEL

I have shed this body ten times.
Tell me the secrets you were never meant to keep,
making a gutter out of my face.
You didn't know you were casting curses, words you meant, like
when you said "I'm ugly" in the mirror.

Tell me the secrets you were never meant to keep.
My whole life, the sound of alone answered.
You didn't know you were casting curses, words you meant, like
when you said "I'm ugly" in the mirror.
I've seen our bodies know forgiveness, maybe why they teach us
how to snore.

My whole life, the sound of alone answered
in every imagination.
I've seen our bodies know forgiveness, maybe why they teach us
how to snore,
watching you vibrate in the sun.

In every imagination
I have shed this body ten times,
watching you vibrate in the sun,
making a gutter out of my face.

OFFERING FROM THE ALIEN

I am from
generations of women
named after flowers
and Black cake.
From women who bent their love into question marks,
such cruelness in second guessing.

I am from men
still digging themselves into
disappearances,

their smallness eclipsing moons,
turning everything soft into eggshells.

I came here to tell you
I wrote these stories

out of an absence—
the shape of
wanting

—and arrived on the other side
crying in bird.

This is the day
the Earth has made,

the day I was born Black,
christened girl,

branded boy in bliss.

Blossom grave,

this is for the band
-stand that broke me

into protecting myself like
suburban holiday lawns from the HOA.

Thank you for being here
even if by accident.

I know you're not one to feed yourself first.

There is so much life
after all it took to get here.

Have a plate.
Eat with both hands.

PART III: A LONG WAY FROM FLORIDA

CUVIER'S BEAKED WHALES HOLD THE RECORD FOR LONGEST BREATH HELD

There is an island of lost left socks
guarded by a troll
who only likes himself when the lights are off.

I'll take the bus with you
to a world away from here
because I have nowhere else to go.

After 10,220 days,
I arrive to the other side of the island alone,
trying to be perfect, the starting line set to bearable.

Everyone understands

I spent the length of closing credits
looking out the window
waiting for a parachute

wrestling with a lake of ruminations.
I believed there was nothing brighter
on the other side of the ripple.

The answer is terrifying

but it taught me how to stop my heart
from breaking how it did.

The answer reminded me
that one day
I woke up

to the sound of my name
in a cadence
sweeter than botanical gardens—

the day I chose to live my life
in fluent whale,
breathing in lighthouse mercy.

THIS IS A POEM FOR PEOPLE WHOSE MOTHERS FORGET THEIR BIRTHDAYS

It all started with saying out loud
what I wanted
to the nightlight:

>To be looked at like a staryard,

>deserving of a love that backlights
>answers like drive-ins.

>An extra day of magic.

>To run on impossibility.

>To be so loved through this loneliness.

The belly of the whale
swallowed on repeat
over the first true lie I was taught:

I am worth
less.

They don't tell you in school that
the hardest part of being human, loving
humans,

is trying to understand
why the neurons of our brains
tell us to break

our bodies.
In a gay bar,

our value
in an undone family,

an *I love you*
after a fight so bad my tongue set the Christmas tree on fire.

Everything collapses parallel
to ocean floor,
Earth looking for mother—

aren't we all?

I grew a garden out of everything
that terrified her.

Branded a poem in the grass for December
when she forgets where I came from.

A prayer too big for belief.

When I say the worst thing that ever happened to me
was figuring out I'm not made up of bad parts,

I meant to say

the more honest I was about my mom

the worst it felt,

that I could do everything right

and I'd still be dressed up like pain
for Halloween with the sun at full exposure.

My family
prefers to put pain to sleep with misdirection.

My family
can't ever stop hurting me.

It's not their fault

their confettied trauma
litters everything cerulean.

I've lost so many people to becoming.

When tears come, I eat my backbone
to remember what it felt like to be held.

I am so big up close it hurts,
born caged,
crying out in particle,
banging to get free.

The question and flatline;
the few places a poem can come from.
I came here to tell you
the day I surrendered, I saw between air.

There is so much hope in a scream.
This bass comes from something
rooted beyond spine,
made of whispers older than alligators.

The dust that said, *become,* to bone.
From the African who said, *enough,* and jumped into the
Atlantic.

This scream is of the beach I would run to as kid
and ask why
I'm here.

I am here.

Raised with low light,

a confession
that has taken years to breathe out,

to tell my mother
I love her

and mean it in fluent complication

with a grief so big
it silences the syllables for home.

INTERSTELLAR

A small Pride flag
planted in potting soil on our balcony;
if it were up to my partner
we'd gift wrap the place in technicolor and mushrooms.

*There was a woman killed this week
over a flag*, she tells me.

I respond with the story of a Black man
murdered at a gas station
for voguing to Beyoncé.

From the sky
you can't see that I triple check the locks
on the doors and windows,

nightlights strategically placed in every corner
because I shake at night.

When my lover's out of town
I booby trap myself in our bedroom.

You'll need infrared to see me from the clouds,
see all the fluorescent in my veins.

I wish we were interstellar,
armed with darkness so deafening
we couldn't hear what our loved ones say when no one's
looking.

I've been freefalling ever since the first word,

collecting flames.
I know myself well enough to know
I come back from ashes.

Love, for the long run,
builds a home out of growing pains,
hardwires every tear into the sockets of your jaw.

My home is unbelievable
in the way she hid rainbows in the carpets,
behind the puzzles
and in my name.

SISTERS

I once heard
you are not a poet
if you don't start
a poem with—

   I.

When you were born
I ripped a hurricane down
the hallway tile,
told everybody with an earlobe
my sister was here,

understood what it meant
to belong to somebody,
woke you up from naps
to remind you I was here,
imagine with you every way
the Earth tries to make sense.

Now I cannot find you
through your depression,
a fog in every answer
I am trained to know,

holding out
that you'll find your way back
to a love that chooses you.
I chose you
from the moment
a part of my name became yours.

II.

I am trying
to reach you in anime,
powered-up children
punching for god,
an earnest question.

I can be someone of value.
I am of value.
I am still learning how

suffering can be a conscious choice,
hoping you'd find yourself
in the story of how I got here,
undoing the ways playing small
may keep your truest self safe.

ME: A COUNTRY

A land invaded
by syringes, white-coated militia, and pigs,
founded by immigrants who had no other choice.
Its early years: a famine,
razed by war.
The capital
is an empty house.
Native tongue:
madness.

Our currency is honesty;
taxes are high.
Every school year the kids are taught in English
how to not make themselves the center of everyone else's story.
In Science, they talk about what happens
when an unstoppable force meets an immovable object,
what to do if that force is love.

Twice a week I am interviewed about this place, my home.
Everyone is scared
of the dark, especially when the lights are on.
The only law of our land is to breathe.
The crime rate is so high we've weaponized every citizen with CPR,
arrests everywhere.

All the residents have the same name
because we believe in making it statistically impossible
not to fall in love
with yourself.

Our flag is the image of an abandoned beach
with the number '2' floating on the waves.
Every morning before our eyes even know they are open,
we must ask ourselves two yes-or-no questions:

1. Is my life happening *to* me or *for* me today?
2. Am I going to run?

ALL THESE LINES WERE KILLED TO MAKE SOMETHING YOU'D LIKE
(Zombie Poem)

I grew up underneath Georgia
a clown car accordion,
gasping trumpet,
emergency room
slow dance with a rope.

In one moment
sitting in a pub that's pretending to be Irish
watching two men argue at the bar about
water or the internet.

In another
I tell my therapist I want to die
because I believed it was the only thing
I would ever be in love with.

Pleading my case with phantoms,
shredding negative self-assessments
made of sweaters too big for my body.

I was not born a consequence.
The Earth loved me back, green
enough to keep it from choosing
whatever natural disaster comes after us.

A sprinkled core,
water balloon exhaling,
it was amazing
the way you whispered my name,
rubbed my chest.

Breathing is an honest poem
like still learning how to sleep
without putting the weight
of a child's wishing well on my shoulders.

I've been kissed
by the moon too many times
to keep apologizing
for being here.

I have a 100% approval rating
from all my mistakes.
There are so many letters left to write,
addressed to the days that went dark.

I'm not asking for god.
There are bigger things than freedom.
There is more at stake here
than falling in love.

CONVERSATION WITH MY ESTRANGED BROTHER BEFORE HURRICANE MILTON

Don't drown
in the storm, please.
Swim.

I left.

Still,
swim.

WHAT IT'S LIKE TO BE A STEALTHY FAG:

Which of the following memories occurred closest to a grocery store?

    A) Suspended against a dirty wall,
       jeans unbuckled, cold belt clinking,
       hot air hands palm bald head—
       Maybe someone sees us.

    B) The older man says,
       I am getting goose bumps just talking like this.

                        Which of the following memories was in reference to
                                              hometowns?

                                    A) Suspended against a dirty wall,
                                        jeans unbuckled, cold belt clinking,
                                        hot air hands palm bald head—
                                        Maybe someone sees us.

                                          B) The older man says,
                         I am getting goose bumps just talking like this.

ODE TO BLACK BOYS, PREVIOUSLY BLACK GIRLS, CALLED OREOS

Donald Glover
was the first Black boy I hid.

Maybe I am him,
already was him,
maybe I ate him.

I hid my love in secret noise.
Couldn't be childish, couldn't play about
a Black man that white boys liked.

The first time I used the n word
I giggled,
rickety like a beach house flash flood,

my skinfolk
erasing every letter,
punctuating with every fence jumped.

I knew witnessing
when Beyoncé declared (as she does),
If you don't have to jump to put jeans on
then you don't know my pain.

Goddamn,
my shower curtain
never seen
a sexier thing
than my ass.

Ask my lover,
tell them
I meant every swinging word.

I murdered my girlhood
by way of girl groups and video vixens.
Can you blame me?
Every hip,
belly button,
flick-wristed dead stare.

Before I knew my shame
I knew my name would never be *Child*.

It would be *Sha-nay-nay*
and the ways both sides stenciled me as

OtherNotEnoughBuckTeethDykeFaggotFreakNerdScaryWhite
WhyYouTalkLikeThat?WhyYouSoQuiet?YouDon'tLikeRapM
usic?YouLikeWhitePeopleMusic?WhyYouReadSoMuch?YouT
akingYourCommunityWithYouScholarshipKidGhettoBrokeNi
ggaNiggerGirlBoySomethingTrannyTravestiteTransexualSlutPr
edatorPreyOtherNotEnoughBuckTeethDykeFaggotFreakNerdS
caryWhiteWhyYouTalkLikeThat?WhyYouSoQuiet?YouDon't
LikeRapMusic?YouLikeWhitePeopleMusic?WhyYouReadSoM
uch?YouTakingYourCommunityWithYouScholarshipKidGhet
toBrokeNiggaNiggerGirlBoySomethingTrannyTravestiteTranse
xualSlutPredatorPrey.

QUEER, AS IN, MY BACKBONE IS

Sweaty bottoms
on the patio
at the dive bar in the Mission,

an angelfish slut
shedding the dead,

scales planted into feet,
repairing all the root rot in tabernacle spirit.

Who gets to tell me I'm beautiful?

To be queer
means I spent a lot of time
looking,

then, now,
sitting out
on the grass
collecting dew.

I rest, bloodied bone.

PART IV: MY BODY & OTHER STORIES PUT TO REST

BANNERLINE RINGLEADER

"...the way you talk
about your transness
is like the drums...but there's a piano
and a guitar and a singer...and a trumpet, maybe. I don't know,
you pick the instruments..."

—A True Story

GRAYSON

My therapist and I have corresponding names.
I think of our sessions as a variety show:

The Two Graysons,
Grayson & Grayson,
What Would Grayson Say?

In therapy
I learned about no longer teaching people how to love me,
that love doesn't come with hesitation.
I learned about magic.

I ran away to a small town in a valley
after trying and failing
to die.

I learned I steal from myself
all the chances I could've taken
to let people know I loved them, truly,
and how, sometimes, there may have been
many people trying to get through to my insides.

I was somebody
who felt like a wanted poster for home,

like hot airing a winter cabin, like someone else
would be the gravity moving my feet,

like I wasn't the moon,
like I didn't collect solar systems around my waist,

like I wasn't every shape of mercy
in a murder house.

I imagine there is someone here who has felt
the same. Maybe it was toxic

or an extended train crash,
but that was me
and so many little pieces in between.

My therapist taught me how all those truths can be.

Me, who I thought was a walking error.
Me, a recovering character assassinator.

My therapist is a workaholic
and a baker.
He is a writer,
drives a truck,
fosters children,
likes fashion,
smiles real big.

I am unlearning the compulsion
to desiccate into boxes of shame
after looking too hard at myself.

I am learning how to unimagine my therapist as perfect
just to qualify him as possible
for caring about me.

Like after I tried killing myself
or like the last time

I went to the hospital.

I want to say
I'm sorry
for leaving him alone
with all my grief,

but I know he'd just tell me,
as easy as ocean,

Don't apologize for having feelings.

MY 9-YEAR-OLD NIECE TOLD ME
SHE KNOWS WHAT A HAIKU IS

      I.
      Maggie is white. Kim
      you are not wrong to ask. It
      is quite concerning.

                           II.
              Don't worry about
              if your dad was loved as a
              dear young child. You are.

      III.
      Do not feel sorry
      for calling me a neutral
      Barbie. You're not wrong.

IV.
No one believed me
when I said I was a boy.
Now, you do. Thank god.

THE BOY WHO DJS THE RIVER

Your grandmother murdered
a large crawling thing
in front of me.

She didn't flinch
as she stomped
and kicked
the flailing carcass.

Your mom loved our salad,
asked for the vinaigrette recipe,
hummed each syllable of cumin,
washed every dish into a pearl,
sang a tune about how everything has changed:

the cupboards,
the fire.
Where does death live?

I washed my ass
by the river,
two-fingered flaming s'mores.

Your sister, crop-topped in Levi shorts,
organizing a five-person fridge
with beer and seltzer.
We lost the frozen corn.
She blew me kisses from the water.

In every moment that cores
this memory,

your grandfather
plays your music
full volume to drown us
out on the deck
as he checks his blood sugar levels,
slapping his palm on the table,
saying your name.

You are loved
in every cabin corner
that curves the font of your name
on the trout placard.

You are alive,
bold-jawed,
no autocorrect,
on purpose and pining.

PORTRAIT OF DATING MEN

Call me inexperienced,
but when you apologized
for the size of your *material*

I forgot there are people who still measure themselves
by how many hands have glittered their body.

Your idea of a date was a cave
of a sports bar,
frozen cock-
tails and room-
temperature hot dogs.

That was all the size I needed
to remember the worth of my desire.

FROM THE THERAPY ROOM

*"This is flesh,
I am flesh."*

*"Is this just part of being a teenager
or is it something else?"*

"Do people just feel things for no reason?"

"Thank you for checking in."

"I'm not Black like you are Black."

"Wait...you're trans?"

"I need to feel safe."

"You're really good at your job."

"Your name is therapy dude *in my phone."*

UPON LEARNING MY FAVORITE PLANET IS THE ONLY ONE WITH A HEART
(Tombaugh Regio)

The shuttle that found the organ
called the New Horizons,
named the region
after Clyde, who left Earth
by way of congenital heart failure.
Maybe he was on Pluto
the whole time.

Chambers said,
*It's a long way
to a small, angry planet.*

Every person clean
as the inside of a prescription bottle—
orange, empty,
safety locking,

born crooked
orbiting in superseasons.

I was a possibility dream,
immigrant hope imagination,
ten-fingered gestational trauma survivor,
most punctured planet
in the broken system.

I couldn't make sense
of the smallest boy
abandoned,
can't hear him wailing

in zero god
from California

for his mother,
for someone to call him
from the scene of becoming.

Pluto
is the only planet
with a pulsing heart.

What, humans thought
he wasn't big enough to fit in the family?

MY LAST GRANDFATHER HAS DIED

No more complicated man bone archivist stories
to know of me, the granddaughter
and the grandson.

No more complicated man bone archivist
to remember I became a man.
Death or cancer or dementia
took all memory of me.

No more complicated man bones
for me to study,
to make sense of my family's brokenness.

No more complicated man fathers
to counter my goodness.

No more complicated
reference checks
for my man bones,
no more stories.

There are no more fathers
to remember
how I got here,
to see, in disruption,
how I drip.

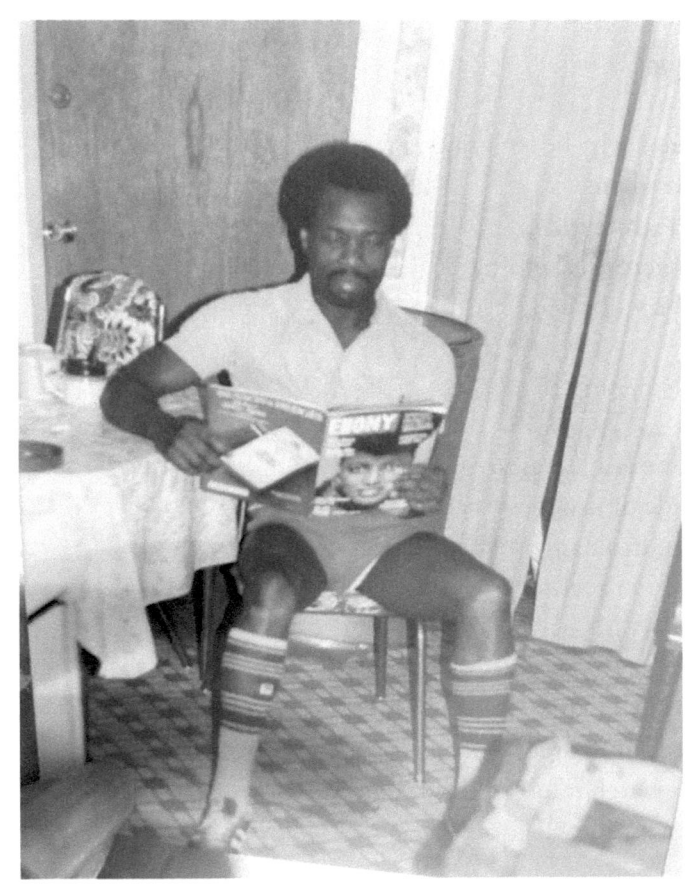

ELECTION (S)KIN

He hates her
name.

That's why he isn't saying it.
The silence
of a white man,
dangerous, claiming
to be wounded,

is drowning.

There is a Jamaican girl
inside of my chest scars,
born in a name that whiteness
made a mockery of.

What a thing
to hear a name
leered at for years
and watch it look like whiteness
with its laugh.

THE BLOWER'S CHILD

A 2023 study suggests
if we leave leaves to coat everything,
if we're honest about winter in decomposition,
then the Earth, and all that we couldn't carry,
will come back stronger.

There is so much life
under our boots after marching
this evisceration dance.
Living can put us through
so much leaf calling
from where your roots came from.

In the 70s, two cities banned leaf blowers
for all the grief crying out the gasket.

Imagine
someone living inside of us
filling that machine,
eating all of that birth,
sucking to get full on pain,
its emptiness the shape of fallout,
sheltering our collective bloom.

I would hide
inside this true-hearted
trumpet shell of a jazz riot
beach sleeping ocean hair
Black goldenrod sweet grass,
tongue out, twerking in the summer,
beautiful.

This body
full of syllables as stilettoed as Megan Thee Stallion
when suffering made a constellation out of her bones.
This body as disassembled as Mychal, the Black librarian a
county away
who got bullied on the internet
for doing everything right,

for trying to fill that emptiness shape
with library cards,
with tattoos and afros,
with poetry.

NOAH AND KATELYN'S LATE WEDDING POEM

Your love is a swallowing
sunset.

When I first met you
you were standing side by side,
floating buoys,
a magnetism as thin as linen.

It never arrived in noise.
It was in your hands,
how they looked so good together.

You are in on the big questions,
the dancing that lives
in the empty space,

the extra stuff that believes
it can grant you permission.

You didn't ask to love like this,
but deserved it
like the truth.

You are a house
with no walls.
Look at all the light,

every dark thing eating its own fear.

Thank you for always giving grace,
for not leaving me the only adventuring ship.

This life didn't know
what it was doing
when it created the way you sound
when you talk to each other,

how your laughter finishes each other's notes.

There is an ultramarathon
for every mile you've marked,
a room full
of pillowtalking
turning TV into chatter,
floating hair
brushed through every room,
testing time gray,
every minute sat in silence
cross-legged on a chair,
leaning through book spines,
building fantasy maps out of a van ceiling.

Don't fly when the bird catches sight.
Hold this dance another spin.

Forgive life for not knowing
it was holding its breath when you met.

It explains all the snow—
freezing each other whole,
vow for vow.
Only forever holds seasons this good.

JOY CAME AFTER THE PRE-REQUISITE COURSES
(For little E, who asked his mom how she knew she was a girl, so she asked her friends)

Girls felt

footloose
and furl,
pink
and pain.

The first word was rage.
Everything after was Scrabble,
everything in me, a crooked painting,
an orbiting mindhouse.

My boyness suspended in apologies,
best dressed for family.
I latched shame to my earlobes
and they told me I was so pretty.

Me, an impatient daydream
in a life stuck in baggage claim,
the origin story of becoming.

I didn't think there were girls like me
who felt sad at everything green.

I am so sorry

you are growing up
in a world filled with leftovers,
of people with missing parts.

You came out
just the way you should,
feeling every injury,
lemon juice fileting our tenderness.

We're all made up of stardust,
big bangs around a table
making sense of microwaved fettuccine.

I still don't know what being a boy feels like,

but I know it felt most like praise
when my reflection wasn't the worst company,
when the scars wrote *cry*
across my chest,
no longer terrified of what girls had.

A rage that evaporates whispers,
undoing everything we project
to protect ourselves
from being held.

I've been a mountain of mouth guards
custom fitting all the hardest parts inside,
breaking the back of any truth trying to echo,
a rubble of letting go,
a rebellion of memories.

I have 35,460 miles of grief behind me
and baby, it's beautiful when you look at it
without blinking.
I made mistakes in big font
to come here and tell you

the words in our heads don't know
the difference between cursing and spelling,
all the wishes for future are already on our lips.

This life that chose me
gave me a blessing in swallowing me whole.
Showed me that true mercy, my honest recovery,
began with telling myself an unbearable truth—

I love you—

forcing each syllable in
until everything I touched,
everything I fucked,
everything I knew
had to make the same choice,

say it again.

CUÍDASE, MAS O MENOS

There's a wizard at the end of bowling lanes
holding prayers between the gutters.

I've been to the answer
behind the pins,
the godhouse
in blacklight bruise.

This strange place,
its strangeness with me,

my personal Chicago. Thank you
for the pizza. Alanis crop-topped saying
in Spanish, *Be careful*.

We were busy yelling around
about our dangerously good time.

No shoes in the house
older than Disney magic.
Patricia asks if there are goblets at the reading for her wine.

You look so pretty
hole punched like that,

thank God no one killed you.

Donika introduced us to her family,
Arkansas down bad, Iowa jeweled.
Celine is singing from a corner I cannot remember,
looking at Roger in a jazz club howling

your name.

You are everywhere,
whiskey and shirtless
in the doorway
plotting and industry
laughing in a cadence only writers understand.

Alex was cradled
by a deflating mattress,
Jesus in the manger
covered in smoke.

MY MOM MAY READ MY POEMS AND NOT KNOW HOW TO BE PROUD OF ME
see "rockaway" by Beres Hammond

If doubling down was a person,
I'd like you to meet my mom.

She is stubborn,
doesn't rest,
runs on a wheel
accelerating out of her body.

Her hands
smell like time,
cold leather, onions, and garlic,
the soil
of where she comes from.

I don't know if she knows where home is anymore.
She never said much about how she got here,
who she was before she changed her name to
Mom.

I was with my mom when the news said
Aaliyah died in the plane crash
then Left Eye in a car crash.
I was next to her in New York when the towers collapsed
and I asked her if the captain would kill us.

Her middle baby,
hiding herself away,
trying to fill this hollow shape.
She watched her youngest
baby's urine fill the toilet black.

She put me on a bus to Maine
because I asked her for adventure,
watched Emeril Lagasse.

BAM!
                                                                         BAM!
                          BAM!

She didn't laugh when I said I wanted to become a chef,
ate every omelet I made, custom to order.

She never questioned the hollow I made
out of the closet corner
where I read every escaping book.

Called me intelligent and inquisitive,
told me I asked too many questions.

I still ask too many questions.

I heard her when she said she was depressed,
every pained sigh with age.
I heard her reject the brainstorm
of ways she could take better care
like therapy, moving her body
for something other than labor,
stop sleeping with the news on.

I watched my mom
become a cake decorator,
learn to drive a car,
say *enough* to every awful man,

eat less so we could have more,
get a high school diploma,
be an imperfect person,
sit alone in the living room,
listen to Shania Twain,
the soundtrack to Grease,
the Bee Gees,
Celine Dion.

My mom, asking me for my hand
in front of the fish tank audience of angelfish
smiling louder than a church bell, yelling,

Dance with your muma!

We watched recordings of *Olivet At Large* with
where she taught me about the history
of our country, of art and pantomime.

In high school, she missed every play
and choir concert, missed my solo
and my trio singing Boyz II Men with a white boy.
She had to work or girls needed care
or that private school made her feel small,
those people who made me feel small.

Or, like in the end of Titanic,
maybe there really wasn't enough room
for both of us,
and maybe, maybe my mother
chose me.

Mom, I always wanted to be where you were,
where you came from.

Beres Hammond
in the car singing,

*remember the songs / used to make you rock away /
those were the days
when love used to reign, hey / we danced all night /
to the songs they played
weekend come again / do it just the same, hey*

Acknowledgements

I want to give a huge shout out to the following literary magazines for creating a home for my writing; each acceptance brought me to this full-length collection. Thank you for keeping poetry alive and choosing my work to be part of your literary stories. In this body of poems, a specific thank you to *Beyond Words* whose publication of "I love you" launched a series of poems for me about desire, and *Foglifter Press*, both for nominating me as winner of the 2024 Start A Riot! Chapbook Prize and for publishing "joy came after the pre-vinylrequisite courses (for E)" for in the Fall 2024 Issue.

I want to share specific gratitude for:

Andrea Gibson: For holding all our hope.

M: You imagined over a decade ago that I could be here, writing with the amazing group of poets I have met and shared words with. You were the first to speak "believe" into my work, to dare me to dream. In many ways, I wrote through all of this to reach you out there somewhere. What I came here to say was this: thank you.

My Therapist: Kellen, you have saved my life. I am a healthier and better person for knowing you. You are one of the best people I know.

My Homies: Wherever you are, thank you for being here.

Butcher Writer Crew: We did it fam.

Suanny Barales: Because Venmo is still not enough.

Buddy Wakefield: "Throwing Crowbirds" started me on a journey for the answer, for forgiveness, for all the life after survival. Then I met you and you told me my poems weren't god awful. Then you asked me why I wrote. Then we became family.

My Family: What a thing, huh?

Gabby Fluke-Mogul: For every median surfed.

Exhibit B: I started believing again when we convened in that creepy AirBnB.

Marguerite Elisabeth Scott: Thank you for everything, all of it, every part it took to get here.

ABOUT THE AUTHOR

Grayson Thompson is a Black, Jamaican American, queer trans cowboy poet, moonlighting as a therapist. A mouthful, Grayson is winner of Write Bloody's 2024 Jack McCarthy Book Prize and Foglifter Press' 2024 Start A Riot! Chapbook Prize for *Sand Bodied Florida Boy*. He's been featured in Cathexis Northwest, Cleaver, Poetry Online, and other homes for poetry. During the 2024 AWP Conference, Grayson opened for the amazing Donika Kelly with Chicago's Exhibit B. Grayson is a TA for Buddy Wakefield's Writer's Anonymous, supporting emerging and established word assemblers. A wanderer, he lives in Northern California. He chooses madness, honest, and full-hearted. He hopes you can find some in his poems.
Instagram to discover their latest projects and creative offerings.
@graysonwritespoems

www.graysonwritespoems.com

IF YOU LIKE GRAYSON, GRAYSON LIKES:

Andrea Gibson
Buddy Wakefield
Noah Arhm Choi
Hieu Minh Nguyen
Anis Mojgani

Discover the beautiful pulse of American poetry at Write Bloody— an indie publisher entirely dedicated to amplifying the voices that crush it on the page and command stages from coast to coast. We transform groundbreaking poets and legends of verse into beautifully crafted books. We love poems that leap off the page with the same intensity the poet's bring to microphones in bars, theaters, and festivals nationwide. Award-winning artists who've toured internationally, our roster represents the most dynamic, diverse and fearless voices reshaping contemporary poetry.

Visit
www.writebloody.com
and join a movement where poetry isn't just read—it's lived, breathed, and performed with unapologetic passion.

SOME OF OUR TITLES:

After the Witch Hunt — Megan Falley
Aim for the Head: An Anthology of Zombie Poetry — Rob Sturma, Editor
Amulet — Jason Bayani
Any Psalm You Want — Khary Jackson
Atrophy — Jackson Burgess
Birthday Girl with Possum — Brendan Constantine
The Bones Below — Sierra DeMulder
Born in the Year of the Butterfly Knife — Derrick C. Brown
Bouquet of Red Flags — Taylor Mali
Bring Down the Chandeliers — Tara Hardy
Ceremony for the Choking Ghost — Karen Finneyfrock
A Choir of Honest Killers — Buddy Wakefield
A Constellation of Half-Lives — Seema Reza
Counting Descent — Clint Smith
Courage: Daring Poems for Gutsy Girls
Dear Future Boyfriend — Cristin O'Keefe Aptowicz
Drive Here and Devastate Me — Megan Falley
Drunks and Other Poems of Recovery — Jack McCarthy
The Elephant Engine High Dive Revival — Derrick C. Brown, Editor
Everyone I Love Is a Stranger to Someone — Annelyse Gelman
Everything Is Everything — Cristin O'Keefe Aptowicz
Favorite Daughter — Nancy Huang
The Feather Room — Anis Mojgani
Floating, Brilliant, Gone — Franny Choi
Glitter in the Blood — Mindy Nettifee
Gold That Frames the Mirror — Brandon Melendez
The Heart of a Comet — Pages D. Matam
Heavy Lead Birdsong — Ryler Dustin
Hello. It Doesn't Matter. — Derrick C. Brown
Help in the Dark Season — Jacqueline Suskin
Hot Teen Slut — Cristin O'Keefe Aptowicz
How to Love the Empty Air — Cristin O'Keefe Aptowicz
I Love Science! — Shanny Jean Maney

I Love You Is Back — Derrick C. Brown
The Incredible Sestina Anthology — Daniel Nester, Editor
In Search of Midnight — Mike McGee
In the Pockets of Small Gods — Anis Mojgani
Junkyard Ghost Revival — Derrick C. Brown, Editor
The Last American Valentine — Derrick C. Brown, Editor
The Last Time as We Are — Taylor Mali
Learn Then Burn — Tim Stafford & Derrick C. Brown, Editors
Learn Then Burn Teacher's Guide — Tim Stafford & Molly Meacham
Learn Then Burn 2: This Time It's Personal — Tim Stafford, Editor
Love in a Time of Robot Apocalypse — David Perez
The Madness Vase — Andrea Gibson
Multiverse: Rob Sturma & Ryk McIntyre, Editors
My, My, My, My, My — Tara Hardy
The New Clean — Jon Sands
New Shoes on a Dead Horse — Sierra DeMulder
No Matter the Wreckage — Sarah Kay
Oh God Get Out Get Out — Bill Moran
Oh, Terrible Youth — Cristin O'Keefe Aptowicz
1,000 Black Umbrellas — Daniel McGinn
Open Your Mouth like a Bell — Mindy Nettifee
Ordinary Cruelty — Amber Flame
Our Poison Horse — Derrick C. Brown
Over the Anvil We Stretch — Anis Mojgani
Pansy — Andrea Gibson
Pecking Order — Nicole Homer
The Pocketknife Bible — Anis Mojgani
Pole Dancing to Gospel Hymns — Andrea Gibson
Racing Hummingbirds — Jeanann Verlee
Reasons to Leave the Slaughter — Ben Clark
Redhead and the Slaughter King — Megan Falley
Rise of the Trust Fall — Mindy Nettifee
Said the Manic to the Muse — Jeanann Verlee
Scandalabra — Derrick C. Brown
Slow Dance with Sasquatch — Jeremy Radin
The Smell of Good Mud — Lauren Zuniga

Songs from Under the River — Anis Mojgani
Strange Light — Derrick C. Brown
38 Bar Blues — C.R. Avery
This Way to the Sugar — Hieu Minh Nguyen
Time Bomb Snooze Alarm — Bucky Sinister
Uh-Oh — Derrick C. Brown
Uncontrolled Experiments in Freedom — Brian S. Ellis
The Undisputed Greatest Writer of All Time — Beau Sia
The Way We Move Through Water — Lino Anunciacion
We Will Be Shelter — Andrea Gibson, Editor
What Learning Leaves — Taylor Mali
What the Night Demands — Miles Walser
Working Class Represent — Cristin O'Keefe Aptowicz
Workin' Mime to Five — Dick Richards
Write About an Empty Birdcage — Elaina Ellis
Yarmulkes & Fitted Caps — Aaron Levy Samuels
The Year of No Mistakes — Cristin O'Keefe Aptowicz
Yesterday Won't Goodbye — Brian S. Ellis

www.ingramcontent.com/pod-product-compliance
Lightning Source LLC
Chambersburg PA
CBHW020625090526
44586CB00049B/698